I0817501

THE POCKET Kimchi

Published in 2025
by Gemini Books
Part of Gemini Books Group

Based in Woodbridge and London

Marine House, Tide Mill Way,
Woodbridge, Suffolk IP12 1AP
United Kingdom

www.geminibooks.com

Part of the Gemini Pockets series

Cover illustration by Clare Owen
Text by Laura Goodwin

ISBN 978-1-80247-286-8

A CIP catalogue record for this book is available from the British Library.

Manufacturer's EU Representative: Eurolink Compliance Limited, 25 Herbert Place, Dublin, D02 AY86, Republic of Ireland. admin@eurolink-europe.ie.

Printed in China

10 9 8 7 6 5 4 3 2 1

Picture Credits: 4 / Clare Owen. Shutterstock: 8, 10, 13, 17, 24, 27, 35, 37, 39, 41, 42, 47, 65, 74, 77, 82, 89, 98, 102, 104, 108, 109, 112 / DiViArt; 45 / MoreVector. Adobe Stock: 57 Iuliia; 81, 92 / Maria.Epine; 94, 105 / HS; 100, 101 / pronick; 106 / SOE; 113 / alexandrakuz; 115 / Sketch Master; 127 / designknowledge.

THE POCKET

Kimchi

G:

CONTENTS

INTRODUCTION

Kimchi, the spicy fermented cabbage dish beloved by Koreans, has never been more popular across the globe. Whether you're already a kimchi addict, or have just discovered the joys of fermenting, *The Pocket Kimchi* is for you.

Learn your *baechu* from your *dongchimi* – and how to make a fool-proof classic kimchi. Find out how to tell if your batch is ready – and what to do if it looks like it's about to explode! Discover the importance of *jeotgal* and *gochugaru* in creating the perfect umami flavour, and the science behind why this fermented dish is so good for you.

Let the kimchi adventures begin!

"Kimchi is a verb, not a noun."

Deuki Hong & Matt Rodbard,
***Koreatown* (2016)**

Chapter One
Craving Kimchi
History & culture

"Kimchi: the gift that keeps on giving."

David Chang chef-founder of Momofuku, New York City, *Gourmet Traveller*, 23 July 2021

EARLY ORIGINS OF KIMCHI

Kimchi originally developed in Korea as a way of preserving fresh vegetables so that they would last longer. Vegetables would be packed with salt and buried underground in large brown ceramic pots called *onggi*, where fermentation with naturally occurring lactic acid bacteria gradually created an acidic environment hostile to pathogens.

The first known written reference to kimchi dates back to the 12th century, when it was alluded to in a poem by Yi Gyubo called 'Six Songs on the Family Garden', which advised that radish could be preserved in salt to eat during winter, and fermented in soybean paste for summer.

WHAT IS KIMCHI?

The Codex Alimentarius of International Food Standards (part of the Food and Agriculture Organization of the United Nations) defines kimchi as a product made with Chinese leaf cabbage (specifically *Brassica pekinensis*) that has been trimmed, salted, washed and drained, then seasoned with a mixture of red pepper powder, garlic, ginger and radish.

The cabbage may be sliced, chopped or broken, then fermented in "appropriate containers" that enable fermentation to develop flavour and produce lactic acid.

CHARACTERISTICS OF KIMCHI

- Red colour that derives from the chilli powder
- Hot and salty taste, which may also be sour
- Texture that is fairly firm but also crisp and chewy

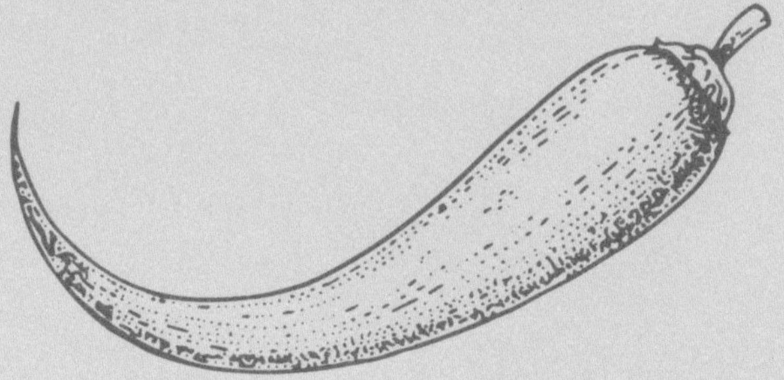

THE RISE OF KIMCHI

Although it has been fundamental to Korean cuisine and culture for centuries, kimchi has only fairly recently gained popularity in the West.

As South Korea industrialized in the 1960s, it experienced speedy economic growth and received more international attention, which propelled kimchi into global consciousness.

Korean restaurants began to proliferate outside the country, and gradually kimchi began to accumulate die-hard fans around the world.

KOREAN WAVE

In the early 2000s, the South Korean government began a gastrodiplomacy mission to promote Korean food and culture (especially kimchi) around the world. This was called *hallyu*, or "Korean wave".

Kimchi's health benefits, and the upsurge in popularity of fermented foods in general, have also helped feed into its global growth.

The boom of other cultural movements out of South Korea – from K-pop and K-dramas to Korean streetwear and esports – accompanied kimchi's rise.

THE HEALTH BENEFITS OF KIMCHI

Kimchi has long been considered one of the healthiest foods in the world. This is because it starts with ingredients that in themselves are high in nutrients, including dietary fibre, amino acids, vitamins, carotenoids, polyphenols, phytochemicals and minerals.

The fermentation process produces many beneficial microbes that have antibacterial and antifungal properties, as well as bolstering the microbiome, with all the benefits that brings to digestion and general health. Some of these are only present in unpasteurized kimchi.

Kimchi has even been found to have lipid-lowering (fat-reducing) effects. The one caveat is its high salt content, which means that excess consumption is not a good idea.

Cabbage, radish, garlic and onion are thought to have anti-inflammatory and anticarcinogenic qualities.

ONGGI

Onggi are earthenware pots that are used for fermenting and storing food and have been used since around 4,000 BCE. They usually have a wide rim and base and a bulbous middle.

They can be patterned or plain, glazed or unglazed, but the fact that they are made from earthenware (rather than stoneware or porcelain) means they are slightly porous and will allow in the small amount of oxygen needed for fermentation.

The craftspeople who make onggi are called *onggijang*.

JANGDOKDAE

A *jangdokdae* is a traditional feature of houses in Korea: an outside terrace or platform designed to hold earthenware jars (onggi) containing stored food or ferments and pickles, including kimchi. In the era before refrigerators this was the best way of keeping the kimchi cool.

The location of the jangdokdae was carefully considered to make best use of the prevailing weather conditions, and the jars were well spaced out to allow air to circulate around them.

TYPES OF KIMCHI

There are thought to be more than 180 different types of kimchi on the Korean peninsula. Opposite are just a few to get you started.

Some have a pickle-like texture and some are more liquid (called *mul* or water kimchi).

Mul kimchi involves submerging the vegetables in a water-based brine and doesn't usually contain jeotgal (fermented seafood paste).

Baechu kimchi – Chinese leaf cabbage

Kkakdugi kimchi – radish

Kkaennip kimchi – perilla (shiso)

Gat kimchi – mustard leaf

Chonggak kimchi – ponytail radish

Oi sobagi kimchi – cucumber

Pa kimchi — green onion

Yeolmu kimchi – young summer radish

Dongchimi – "winter kimchi", a mul kimchi made with small young radishes just before winter

Nabak kimchi – mul kimchi made with radish cut into thin squares and other vegetables and fruit (traditionally pear)

BAECHU (CABBAGE) KIMCHI

Despite being a relative newcomer on the kimchi scene compared to radish kimchi (it did not appear in recipe books until 1766), kimchi made with Chinese leaf cabbage (baechu, also known as napa cabbage) is now by far the best-known form of kimchi outside South Korea. It is also the most ubiquitous type inside the country.

Baechu kimchi is listed in the Codex Alimentarius of International Food Standards as the "standard" form of kimchi.

KKAKDUGI (RADISH) KIMCHI

Kkakdugi kimchi, made with the Korean *joseonmu* radish, is the second most popular type of kimchi in Korea, after baechu kimchi.

Although nowadays the most widely known type of kimchi is made with cabbage, originally most kimchi was made with radish of various types.

Kkakdugi kimchi is made with large square chunks of salted radish coated in a spice paste.

Many Korean families have their own recipes for kimchi that have been passed down through the generations.

Kimchi Heroes #1

Agricultural scientist **Dr Woo Jang-choon** (1898–1959) was instrumental in the development of the commercial cultivation of baechu, or Chinese leaf cabbage, which is the main ingredient of the most popular type of kimchi.

His work on hybrid cultivars and improving seed production meant that varieties of baechu could be produced with greater disease resistance and tolerance of different growing conditions and temperatures. This meant that growers' yields improved immensely.

YAK SIK DONG WON

This traditional Korean phrase translates roughly as "food is medicine"; in other words, food has everything we need for good health.

Traditional Korean cuisine is considered to epitomize this principle through its emphasis on balanced flavours, communal eating, fermented foods and fresh ingredients.

The average Korean eats one ounce (30 g) of kimchi every day – that's 22 lb (10 kg) a year! It's an essential accompaniment to every meal.

"I used to always have my pork pie with either English mustard, or with Branston's [pickle]. Now I have it with kimchi."

Marco Pierre White,
***The Independent*, 22 June 2021**

CANNING KIMCHI

The Vietnam War brought with it an important development in the history of kimchi. To help persuade South Korea to join the war effort against Vietnam, US President Lyndon B. Johnson agreed to help Korea with the preservation of kimchi in cans, so that it could reach Korean soldiers stationed furthest away from the homeland, and help them to withstand jungle conditions.

As well as providing funding, experts from the USA worked with Korean canning factories to improve their procedures and equipment, and long-life kimchi was successfully canned for the first time.

THE KIMCHI MUSEUM

Kimchikan, the museum of kimchi in Seoul, the capital of South Korea, was first opened in 1986 to celebrate the cultural heritage of kimchi and its importance to the Korean people.

Visitors can explore every aspect of kimchi, and even "listen" to the sounds of its flavours in a series of interactive installations and videos.

For a time, there was an outpost of the kimchi museum in Honolulu, Hawaii, but sadly it has since closed.

KIMCHI REFRIGERATORS

So beloved is kimchi in Korea that many households have a dedicated kimchi refrigerator designed to preserve the ferments for as long as possible by creating a more temperature-stable environment than ordinary refrigerators. The cooling element surrounds the food, so that the air does not need to be circulated.

Some models even feature drawers at different temperatures required by kimchis at different stages of the fermentation process.

KIMCHI IN SPACE

Yi So-yeon, the first South Korean astronaut, took a high-nutrition version of kimchi created specially for her by scientists when she undertook her first space mission in 2008. It did not contain any microorganisms, as it was feared that radiation from the sun's rays might cause the bacteria to mutate.

One researcher is said to have stated that "if a Korean goes to space, kimchi must go there too."

"Don't drink kimchi soup thinking that someone will give you rice cakes."

Korean proverb, the equivalent of "Don't count your chickens before they hatch."

THE WORLD'S OLDEST KIMCHI

A stone structure in the shape of a huge earthenware pot was found partially buried near the Beopjusa Buddhist temple, within Songnisan National Park, South Korea.

Archeologists believe it was placed there in 720 and held enough kimchi for thousands of monks.

Burying pots of kimchi in the ground is a great way of maintaining a stable, cool temperature, which is just what it needs to ferment.

KIMJANG

For centuries, Koreans have gathered together in early November to prepare enough kimchi to last through the winter, observing a tradition called *kimjang* (or *gimjang*). This communal ritual shared the workload and ensured that everyone would have enough to eat.

The annual event remains popular and is still observed today. In the central city square in Seoul, the kimchi festival is still attended by thousands of families preparing more than 50 tons (45 tonnes) of cabbage.

In 2013 South Korean kimchi was declared an Intangible Cultural Heritage of Humanity by UNESCO.

Two years later, North Korea received the same recognition for its kimchi (which is less spicy), meaning the dish appears on UNESCO's list twice!

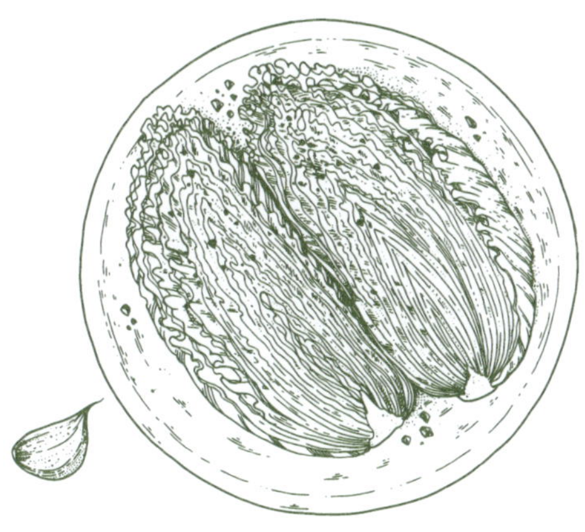

THE WORLD INSTITUTE OF KIMCHI

This august institution, known as WiKim for short, was opened in 2010 as a research and development centre to fund technical innovation in the production of kimchi and promote kimchi culture around the world.

WiKim also works to support domestic kimchi producers and to reduce South Korea's reliance on imports of kimchi from elsewhere (mostly China). Its headquarters are in Gwangju, South Korea's sixth largest city.

More than 90 per cent of South Koreans eat kimchi every day.

REGIONAL VARIATIONS

Kimchis from the northern region of the Korean peninsula tend to contain less salt and have a less pronounced taste. They often don't contain as much chilli, so are lighter in colour. And due to the colder temperatures, fermentation is slower which also contributes to the milder taste.

Kimchis from the south tend to be saltier, spicier and ferment faster. The fermented seafood used also varies from region to region.

KIMCHI WASN'T ORIGINALLY SPICY

Chillies are native to South America and weren't part of the traditional kimchi recipe until they were introduced to Korea in the 17th century by Portuguese traders.

In fact, chilli didn't start to feature regularly in kimchi until the 19th century.

Early records of kimchi don't include garlic either.

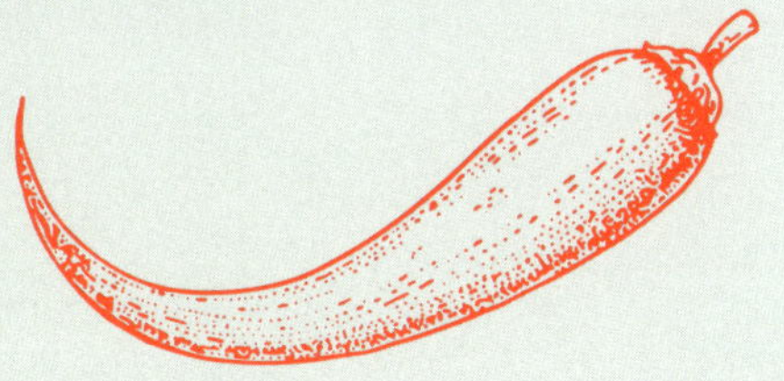

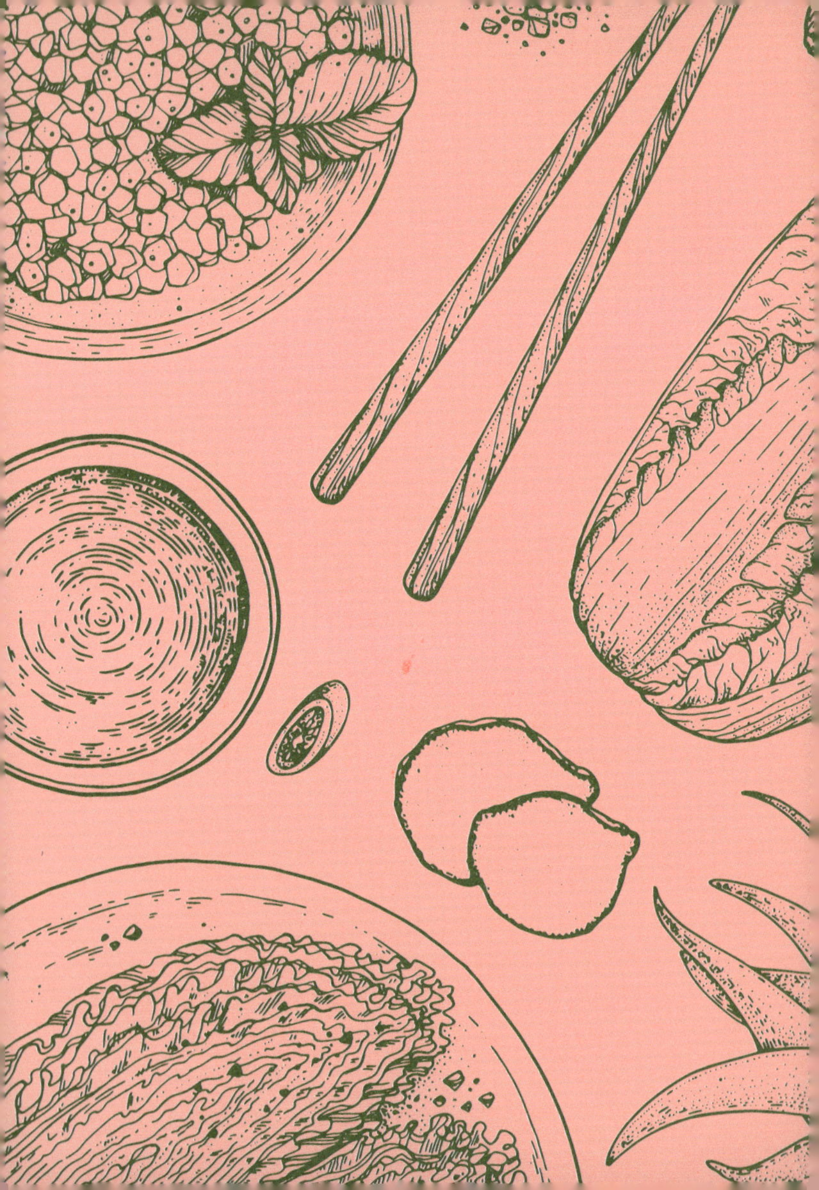

Chapter Two
Making Kimchi
Recipes for the perfect pickle

"'Kimchi' does not describe a single product, but an entire style of Korean vegetable fermentation."

James Read, *Of Cabbages & Kimchi* (2023)

THE KEY STAGES OF KIMCHI

1) Wash and chop the vegetables or fruit.
2) Let them sit in salt, brine or fish sauce for a few hours, until softened.
3) If salt is used, rinse the vegetables well.
4) Coat the vegetables with a flavouring paste, which typically includes gochugaru (Korean chilli flakes), garlic, ginger and jeotgal (fermented shrimp paste).
5) Place the mixture in airtight jars and store at a constant temperature (ideally 40–50°F/ 5–10°C) for a few days, until the desired flavour is reached. Then store in the refrigerator.

BAECHU

The Korean name for the cabbage most often used to make kimchi is baechu. Elsewhere, it's known as Chinese leaf cabbage or napa cabbage. It's a fairly large cabbage with an elongated shape, white ribs and bright green leaves. Some varieties grow up to 18 in (46 cm) long.

Chinese leaf cabbage originated – not surprisingly – in China, where the first records of it being cultivated date back to the 15th century, near the Yangtze River. It grows well in cool conditions; in warmer temperatures it is very quick to flower.

Because South Korea is extremely mountainous, only around 7 per cent of the land can be used for cultivation and the principal crop is rice. It therefore has to import most of its baechu from other countries.

Baechu is high in vitamin C, vitamin K, fibre and minerals.

Its sweet flavour and soft texture make it ideal for making kimchi.

"You need the best ingredients possible, at the height of their freshness, to make delicious kimchi. Make sure your cabbage is vibrant."

David Chang, *Gourmet Traveller*, 23 July 2021

Classic Baechu Kimchi

To make your own kimchi you'll need a chopping board, knife, rubber gloves, large and small nonreactive mixing bowls, colander, large spoon and a sterilized 34 fl oz (1 litre) glass storage jar with a tight-fitting lid. Your bowls need to be glass or stainless steel to avoid imparting any unwanted flavours to the kimchi.

INGREDIENTS

1½ lb (675 g) Chinese leaf cabbage
5½ oz (150 g) Korean white radish, daikon or carrots
5–6 spring onions
1¾ oz (50 g) fine sea salt
5 garlic cloves, roughly chopped
1 in (2.5 cm) fresh root ginger, roughly chopped
¾ oz (20 g) gochugaru (Korean chilli flakes)
1 ½ oz (45 g) red or brown miso paste or ¾ oz (20 g) jeotgal (preserved shrimp paste)

- Cut the cabbage into quarters lengthways, then into wide slices. Wash well in the colander.
- Peel and cut the white radish, daikon or carrots into thin strips. Cut the spring onions into similar strips.
- Separate out the cabbage slices and arrange them and the other vegetables in layers in a mixing bowl, sprinkling sea salt between each layer.
- Cover and leave for several hours or overnight, until the cabbage has softened and reduced in volume.
- Drain off any liquid and rinse the vegetables in cold water, then drain well.
- In a small bowl, grind or blend the garlic, ginger, gochugaru and the miso or jeotgal (whichever you are using) to form a paste.
- Wearing gloves, massage the paste into the vegetables with your hands.

- Spoon the coated cabbage mixture into the jar. Add a weight to make sure the cabbage is submerged in the liquid it produces. Fasten the lid well and leave somewhere cool – not in direct sunlight or near a heat source – for a few days (the warmer the temperature, the faster it will ferment).
- Taste the kimchi every day and, when you're happy with it, transfer it to the refrigerator. If you see lots of bubbles you will need to "burp" the jar regularly to release excess gas.
- You can then eat the kimchi immediately, but the longer you leave it the fuller the flavour will become. It should be eaten within 3–4 weeks.

TIP

Take care to use a clean spoon when serving the kimchi, so as not to introduce germs. If you see mould forming, discard the kimchi.

TEMPERATURE

Opinions vary on the best temperature for storing kimchi, but what kimchi makers aim for is a stable temperature that's not too hot (which would mean the kimchi ferments quickly and becomes very sour and single-note in flavour) and not too cold (which would mean it ferments too slowly and the texture of the vegetables would change too much).

A temperature of around 50°F (10°C) seems to be a good middle ground, although that's not easy to achieve, which is why avid home kimchi makers often use a special temperature-controlled refrigerator.

TIME

Knowing when your kimchi is ready is a matter of personal preference, and depends on the level of acidity you enjoy, so it's wise to check it regularly.

For quicker results it can be stored at room temperature and should be ready within a few days; it may have a slightly fizzy texture caused by the carbon dioxide that the microbes produce at warmer temperatures.

In the refrigerator it will likely take 2–3 weeks to ferment, and may lose some texture.

You know your kimchi is ready when it changes from raw-tasting to tangy and well-balanced, with less of a strong garlic flavour.

The American Journal of Public Health declared kimchi one of the five healthiest foods in the world, thanks in part to its probiotic *Lactobacillus* bacteria.

"Probiotic" simply means live microorganisms that you introduce to your body to improve your microbiome, and therefore your gut health.

NOT JUST CABBAGE

Although baechu (Chinese leaf cabbage) and radish kimchi are the best-known types, other ingredients can be used in the famous ferment, and there are many regional variations throughout the Korean peninsula. Here are some other ingredients you might find in kimchi:

Salted herring

Aubergine (eggplant)

Blowfish

Pomegranate

Pear

Mustard leaf

Angelica (wild celery)

Seaweed

Chestnut

Mushroom

Shiso (beefsteak plant)

Kimchi Troubleshooting #1

If your kimchi turns slimy and resembles egg whites, give it a sniff. If it still smells like kimchi, it's likely to be a side product of *Leuconostoc* bacteria reproducing too quickly, possibly because the temperature is too high, or there isn't enough salt to regulate the fermentation. It should resolve itself in a day or two.

If it smells weird (in a non-kimchi way), throw it out.

ACIDITY

The optimal acidity level of kimchi when it is ready to eat is between 0.6 and 0.7 per cent, with a pH level of between 4.2 and 4.3.

Taste your kimchi every day, and put it in the refrigerator once it's reached the right level of acidity for you.

JEOTGAL – FERMENTED SEAFOOD

Salted fermented seafood – jeotgal – is a common ingredient in many types of kimchi.

It's an essential but sometimes neglected element that contributes a deep umami savouriness that is the backbone of good kimchi.

There are countless types of jeotgal in Korea, made with different types of seafood, from the basic shrimp to squid, anchovy, oysters, clams, pollock or even sea pineapple (also – less picturesquely – called sea squirt). There's even a type that includes pumpkin, sesame or sunflower seeds for a nutty flavour.

Saeujeot – salted small shrimp

Jogijeot – salted yellow croaker fish

Myeolchijeot – salted anchovies

Galchijeot – salted righteye flounder

Kuljeot – salted anchovy

Changnanjeot – salted pollock intestines and roe

Ojingeojeot – salted squid

Sikhae — salted fish with cooked millet or quinoa grains and chilli, garlic and ginger

TIP

If you prefer not to use jeotgal or Korean fish sauce when making kimchi, soy sauce and/or red or brown miso (not the sweeter white type) can be good substitutes. Or make your own vegan fish sauce (see page 85).

Yeolmu (Summer Radish) Kimchi

This traditional kimchi is made with leafy summer radishes called *yeolmu*. It is often enjoyed just as it is during the summer months, as a kind of cold spiced soup, or mul kimchi. Try to make it with small white radishes with plenty of leafy tops.

INGREDIENTS

2¼ lb (1 kg) small white radishes
5½ oz (150 g) salt
1 tbsp flour
1 tbsp sugar
1 white onion or 3 spring onions (scallions)
3 garlic cloves, minced
1 in (2.5 cm) fresh root ginger, finely chopped
2 red or green chillies, sliced
1 tbsp gochugaru (Korean chilli flakes)
3 tbsp fish sauce or 1 tbsp salt

- Peel the radishes, cut them into long batons and wash them well, along with their leaves.
- Drain, mix in the salt, and let the mixture sit for an hour, turning occasionally. Then rinse and drain.
- In a small pan, make a paste with the flour and 7 fl oz (200 ml) water. Cook over a gentle heat, stirring continuously, until it thickens. Stir in the sugar and set aside to cool.
- Cut the onion or spring onions into thin slices and place in a large nonreactive bowl along with the garlic and ginger, chillies, gochugaru and fish sauce or salt.
- Add the flour paste and the drained radishes and mix well with gloved hands.
- Transfer to a sterilized container with a lid. Leave in a cool place for 1–2 days to kickstart fermentation, then transfer to the refrigerator.

Dongchimi

Dongchimi means "winter kimchi" and is traditionally made with young radishes in autumn, to preserve them for winter. It's milder and more liquid than baechu (cabbage) kimchi; it belongs to the mul or "watery" category of kimchi. Use Korean white radish (joseonmu) if you can find it, or if not, any type of Asian white radish such as daikon.

INGREDIENTS

2¼ lb (1 kg) white radish
1½ oz (45 g) salt
6 garlic cloves, roughly chopped
1 in (2.5 cm) fresh root ginger
10 oz (300 g) Asian (nashi) pear
(or ordinary pear)
3–4 spring onions (scallions)
2–3 long green chillies

- Peel the radish and cut it into half-moon slices about ½ in (1 cm) thick. Mix with the salt in a nonreactive bowl and leave for 1–2 hours.
- Drain off and reserve any liquid. Rinse the radish well in a colander.
- Blend or grind to a paste the garlic and ginger with the pear. Pass this paste through a fine sieve and mix it with the radish liquid.
- Cut the spring onions into 1 in (2.5 cm) lengths. Cut the chillies into short lengths and mix with the spring onions and radish. Pack this into a sterilized jar.
- Fill the jar with the garlic and radish liquid. If the vegetables aren't completely submerged, top the jar up with a 2 per cent salty brine (2 tsp salt to 1 pint (600 ml) water).
- Seal the jar and keep it in a cool place for 2–4 days. When it starts to get fizzy, move it to the refrigerator. Taste it regularly until it reaches a flavour you like. Release the gas every few days.

GOCHUGARU – KOREAN DRIED CHILLI

Gochugaru is dried Korean chilli powder or flakes, and it's widely used in Korean cooking, from *bulgogi* (barbecue) to kimchi.

It has a deep orange-red colour and a sweet, smoky, fruity flavour as well as medium-low heat.

Gochugaru is available at varying levels of grind, from fine powder to chilli flakes. For kimchi it is normally used as fine flakes, which allows the colour to infuse but remain flecked throughout.

Gochugaru ranks at 2,500 on the Scoville Heat Scale.

This is relatively mild when compared with cayenne at 50,000 or Scotch Bonnet, which is 250,000.

SEASONAL KIMCHI

Because it originated as a way of preserving vegetables to be eaten at a time of year when they don't normally grow, kimchi is a seasonal dish, and different types tend to be eaten at different times of year, even though the ingredients are now available more widely.

TIP

Mul (water) kimchi is particularly enjoyed in summertime as a cooling condiment.

Kimchi Troubleshooting #2

If your kimchi goes mouldy, it's probably because the vegetables have been exposed to air and picked up bacteria. You'll have to throw away this batch.

To avoid it in future, make sure the vegetables are submerged in the liquid produced by the fermentation – using weights inside the jar can help with this.

Kkakdugi (Diced Radish) Kimchi

Legend has it that Princess Sukseon of Korea (1793–1836) created this radish kimchi by accident and, upon discovering it tasted good, introduced it to the court, where King Jeongjo named it kkakdugi after the Korean term for cutting ingredients into cubes: *kkakduk seolgi.*

INGREDIENTS

2¼ lb (1 kg) Korean radish
2 tbsp coarse salt
2 tbsp sugar
½ white onion
½ apple, peeled
3 tbsp fish sauce
3 garlic cloves
1 in (2.5 cm) fresh root ginger
1 tbsp rice flour
4 tbsp gochugaru (Korean chilli flakes)
3 spring onions

- Cut the radish into ¾ in (2 cm) cubes and combine it in a mixing bowl with the salt and sugar. Leave it to sit for a few hours.
- Meanwhile, make the kimchi base. Place the onion, apple, fish sauce, garlic and ginger in a small blender and whizz until smooth.
- Mix the rice flour with 3 tbsp water in a bowl and heat over a low-to-medium heat for 1 minute to make a thin rice porridge. Combine this with the onion and apple mixture along with 2 tbsp of gochugaru.
- After the radish has been salted, rinse it well in cold water, then drain. In a large bowl, combine it with the kimchi base, the spring onions cut into short lengths and the rest of the gochugaru.
- Mix well with your hands (wearing gloves), then pack it into sterilized jars and leave in a cool place (not the refrigerator) for 1–2 days. After that, transfer it to the refrigerator. It should be ready after 3–4 more days.

JOSEONMU – KOREAN RADISH

The bulbous white Korean radish (joseonmu) is relatively mild with a crisp, crunchy texture. It looks a bit like daikon (Japanese white radish) but is shorter and more rounded.

The word *mu* can refer to this particular type of radish, or to radish more generally. It's one of Korea's principal crops, and the kimchi made with the flesh is very popular. The green leaves are also often used in cooking too.

CHONGGAKMU – PONYTAIL RADISH

The chonggak radish is named after a distinctive hairstyle traditionally adopted by Korean boys for their coming-of-age ceremony, which consists of two topknots, a bit like horns. The shape of the radish resembles the chonggak hairstyle: cylindrical and about 3 in (7.5 cm) long with a wider, rounded base.

The chonggak radish and its greens are used to make chonggak kimchi or dongchimi.

GEGEOLMU – GEGEOL RADISH

The *gegeol* radish is one of many types of radish prized in Korea. Its thick skin and firm flesh means that it retains its texture in kimchi very well.

Traditionally grown in the Icheon and Yeoju regions in the northern parts of South Korea, it has a particularly strong, peppery flavour. It is used fresh, salted and dried, as well as being made into kimchi. Its leaves are also eaten fresh or dried.

Gegeolmu kimchi is made with diced radish, mustard greens, glutinous rice powder, fish sauce, gochugaru, garlic, ginger, spring onions and plum syrup.

WHY ADD RICE FLOUR?

Some kimchi recipes will include a starch component such as rice flour.

This provides extra food for the beneficial microbes that kimchi depends on, helping to accelerate their growth.

It also helps to thicken the seasonings and binds them to the ingredients to create a fuller flavour.

WILD FERMENTS

Fermented products can be divided into two types:

- Those that need a starter to be added to kickstart the fermentation process (such as sourdough, yoghurt or soy sauce)
- Those that don't, such as sauerkraut and kvass. These use the natural microbes found on the raw ingredients to begin the fermentation.

In kimchi, the ingredient that contributes most to the fermentation process is the garlic, which is thought to contain nearly 100 different bacteria strains, as well as some yeasts. But all the ingredients will have their own varied microbes.

If you were to massage your kimchi the traditional way (with your bare hands), this would also pass on microbes. Wearing gloves will protect your hands from smelling of kimchi, though, which is what we suggest in this book!

Kimchi Heroes #2

BYUNG HI-LIM & BYUNG SOON-LIM

Along with their mother and aunt, sisters Byung Hi-lim and Byung Soon-lim run the restaurant Arirang, in Stockholm, Sweden.

The first Korean restaurant in Scandinavia, and now a celebrated hub for Korean food culture, Arirang opened in 1975 and was one of the pioneers who brought the flavours of kimchi to Western diners.

For the sisters, kimchi is not a dish or a recipe – rather, it's an activity that unfolds over time. Every time the lid of a kimchi jar is opened, the flavours have changed slightly.

"I've become green onion kimchi."

A Korean saying to describe when you feel exhausted and have collapsed on the sofa with no energy. You might look like spring onion kimchi that has lost its firmness due to fermentation!

Brilliant Bacteria #1

Lactobacillus is a genus of bacteria, specifically of lactic acid bacteria, and is an essential element in fermented products such as kimchi.

Lactobacilli help produce kimchi's sour flavour and prolong its shelf life because pathogens cannot survive the acidity.

They are also naturally present in areas of the body including the digestive system, where they help protect against infection from germs.

Research has found that there are more than 12 strains of *lactobacilli* commonly found in kimchi. These include:

Lactobacillus sakei

Lactobacillus graminis

Lactobacillus gelidum

Lactobacillus gasicomitatum

Each strain will contribute varying flavour compounds depending on the ingredients they are interacting with, as well as contributing antimicrobial and antifungal properties at different stages of their life cycles. It's also thought that they help reduce cholesterol levels.

THE FLAVOUR STAGES OF KIMCHI

When the ingredients are first combined, before fermentation begins, it's called *geotjeori*, which is more like a salad or coleslaw and can be eaten like this straightaway.

When it is one to four weeks old, the mixture begins to fizz and acquire its distinctive fermented flavour. This is when most kimchi is consumed.

As it is stored for longer, it becomes gradually more sour. After six months it is called *mugeunji*, and tends to be eaten alongside other strong-flavoured foods that can stand up to its robust flavour, or used in slow-braised pork stews to cut through the richness.

CHAMCHWI – KOREAN ASTER

Chamchwi, also known as Korean aster (*Doellingeria scabra*), is a widespread perennial in East Asia, cultivated in Korea for its medicinal benefits. The stems and leaves are used in cooking as a *namul* (herbal side dish), or alongside pork.

Chamchwi kimchi is a mul (water) kimchi made with a broth that contains liquorice. It is also sometimes used as a flavouring herb in other types of kimchi.

Pa (Green Onion) Kimchi

This spicy and pungent kimchi is slightly easier to make than classic baechu kimchi and makes a nice alternative. For a vegan version, substitute the fish sauce for soy sauce or red or brown miso.

INGREDIENTS

1 lb 2 oz (500 g) spring onions (scallions)
4 tbsp gochugaru (Korean chilli flakes)
4 tbsp fish sauce
½ tsp salt
4 garlic cloves, minced
¾ in (2 cm) fresh root ginger, finely chopped
2 tsp sugar

- Wash the spring onions well, trim them, and cut into 1 in (2.5 cm) lengths, including the dark green bits. Traditionally, they are left whole, but cutting them makes the kimchi a bit easier to handle.
- Make a paste with the gochugaru, fish sauce, salt, garlic, ginger and sugar.
- Massage this paste into the onions (wearing gloves), then pack them into a sterilized storage container.
- Keep in a cool place for 1–2 days, then transfer to the refrigerator.
- Eat whenever it has reached a flavour you like.

KOREAN FISH SAUCE

Fish sauce is an essential component of many Korean dishes, and for some types of kimchi it is used in place of salt to create the conditions for fermentation.

Any type of light, well-balanced Asian fish sauce can be used.

Vegan Fish Sauce

Try making your own vegan alternative to fish sauce. This recipe creates a strongly flavoured, salty, savoury stock with a hint of sweetness.

- In a saucepan, combine 12 fl oz (350 ml) light soy sauce, 2 tbsp each of rice vinegar and mirin (rice wine), 1 tsp oyster mushroom sauce and 1 pint (600 ml) water.
- Add 6 dried shiitake mushrooms, 5 pieces of *kombu* (seaweed), 2 oz (60 g) nashi pear or apple, 2 sliced shallots and 4 garlic cloves.
- Bring to a boil, then simmer to reduce the mixture by half (about 1½ hours).
- Leave to cool, then sieve or strain the mixture. Pour the liquid into an airtight container. It will keep in the refrigerator for up to 3 months.

Vegan Kimchi

Kimchi usually contains fish sauce and/or shrimp paste, which add an umami base note. These can be replaced with soy sauce and/or red or brown miso (not the sweeter white or yellow miso) to create a vegan version.

INGREDIENTS

1½ lb (675 g) Chinese leaf cabbage
2 tbsp flaky salt
8 spring onions (scallions), chopped
8 garlic cloves, minced
2 oz (60 g) gochugaru (Korean chilli flakes)
2 tbsp red or brown miso paste
1 tbsp sugar

- Put the cabbage (leaves separated) in a nonreactive bowl with the salt and spring onions, and toss to coat.
- Leave to sit at room temperature for a few hours, until the cabbage has wilted and released plenty of liquid.
- In a small bowl, mix the garlic with the gochugaru, miso and sugar.
- Once the cabbage has wilted, add the garlic mixture and mix to coat, then add 7 fl oz (200 ml) water.
- Pack the mixture with its liquid into sterilized jars, pressing down to make sure the cabbage is covered.
- Seal the jars and leave at room temperature for a day, then transfer to the refrigerator. It will keep gradually getting sourer; eat it at whatever point you like.

SALT

An essential component of kimchi, salt works by killing off some of the less desirable bacteria, thereby reducing the competition for the good bacteria.

It also puts the brakes on the fermentation and stops it from proceeding too quickly, resulting in the kimchi becoming excessively sour. The end product usually has about 2 per cent salinity.

Koreans have the longest life expectancy (83.5 years) of many developed countries.

Experts believe that this is at least in part thanks to the consumption of kimchi.

Brilliant Bacteria #2

One of the most important strains of microbe for kimchi-making is *Weissella*, usually in the form of *Weissella kimchi, Weissella confusa* and *Weissella koreensis.*

In kimchi, it comes into its own once the *Leuconostoc* species have died away and before the *Lactobacillus* species take over.

Each type of microbe contributes a different flavour profile as well as probiotic benefits to kimchi.

CHAMNAMUL – PIMPINELLA

This plant in the Apiaceae (wild carrot) family is valued for its aromatic leaves, which are often made into kimchi along with the stalks.

Chamnamul is also increasingly used for Korean versions of Western dishes like pesto or pasta, or is served as a vegetable side dish with soy sauce and other flavourings.

It's similar to *mitsuba*, a herb used in Japanese cooking (sometimes called Japanese wild parsley), which is more widely available outside Korea.

Morchovka (Carrot Salad)

Although more of a carrot salad than kimchi, this has many similarities with kimchi. Its origins are Russian, and variants of it are found in many formerly Soviet countries, as well as in Korea.

INGREDIENTS

1 lb 2oz (500 g) carrots
1 tsp flaky sea salt
1 tbsp sugar
2 tbsp rice vinegar
1 tsp gochugaru
(Korean chilli flakes)
3 tbsp vegetable oil
1 tsp ground coriander (cilantro)
4 garlic cloves, minced

- Peel and slice the carrots into thin matchsticks or julienne (you could also grate them coarsely in a food processor).
- Toss the carrot slices with the salt in a nonreactive bowl and set aside for 30 minutes to wilt.
- Add the sugar, vinegar and gochugaru to the carrots and stir well.
- Heat the oil in a pan and add the coriander and garlic.
- As soon as the garlic has sizzled and perfumed the oil, pour the oil and garlic over the carrots and stir well.
- Allow to sit for 1–2 hours, if you can, to let the flavours meld. Then enjoy!

USUKUCHI

Usukuchi is a light style of soy sauce that is fermented for a year or less. Some cooks like to add it to their kimchi seasoning paste to boost the umami flavour.

Other ingredients that boost umami are jeotgal (fermented seafood), fish sauce and miso.

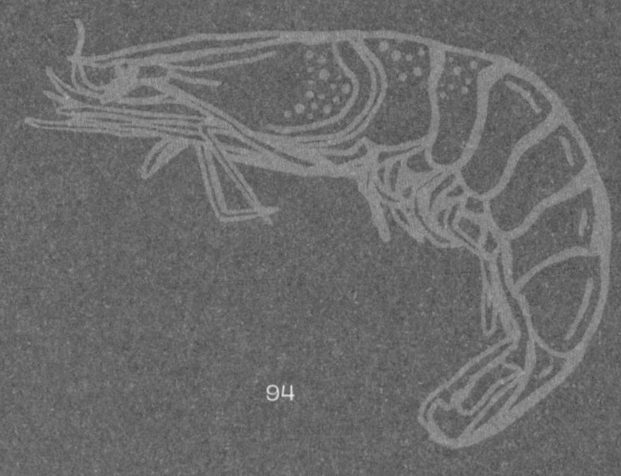

Brilliant Bacteria #3

Leuconostoc is a genus of lactic acid bacteria found in kimchi; one common strain is *Leuconostoc mesenteroides.* It aids fermentation in combination with salt and a low temperature.

Along with other lactic acid bacteria, it helps to produce the flavour compounds unique to kimchi, as well as contributing to its health benefits.

GARLIC

Garlic isn't just important in kimchi for its flavour: it's also crucial in the fermentation process. Garlic naturally contains many strains of "good" bacteria (i.e. the types you want in kimchi), which kick-start fermentation.

Perhaps counterintuitively, it also helps to eradicate microbes linked with foodborne illness, such as *E. coli.*

When the inside of a garlic clove is exposed to the air by cutting, crushing or mincing, it releases a compound called allicin (the same one that produces the smell), which is a natural defence against undesirable bacteria – and being nibbled by insects.

As the kimchi ages, the allicin's effects wane and the garlic becomes less pungent, resulting in a more balanced flavour.

UEONG – BURDOCK ROOT

Also known as greater burdock, *ueong* is a popular kimchi ingredient in Korea thanks to its health-giving properties.

The taproot of a tall plant with distinctive wavy-edged leaves, burdock has a crisp, sweet flavour.

It is valued for its high dietary fibre, good amounts of minerals and amino acids and detoxifying properties. Dried burdock root is also used in traditional Chinese medicine.

NABAK KIMCHI

A relatively mild kimchi made with thinly sliced radishes and Chinese leaf cabbage with garlic and ginger fermented in a salty brine with a little sugar and gochugaru.

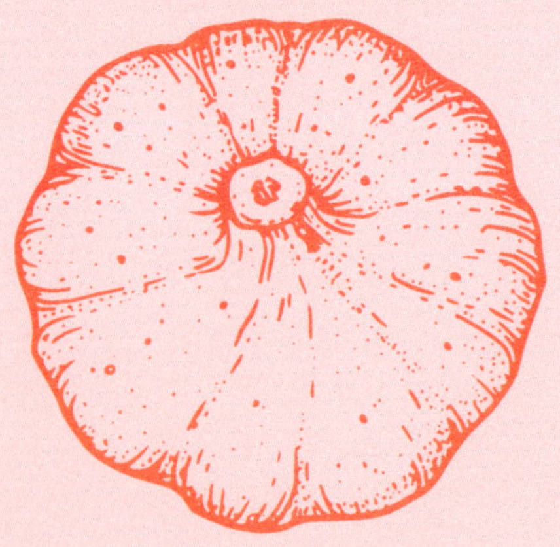

Kimchi Troubleshooting #3

> If your kimchi tastes raw and uninspiring – don't panic! It's just not ready yet.
>
> Give it another day or two, then taste it again. If it still lacks acidity, move it to a warmer area.

"There are few things as satisfying as a big bowl of kimchi and a cold beer."

Anthony Bourdain,
***Kitchen Confidential* (2000)**

Kimchi Troubleshooting #4

If your kimchi looks like it's about to explode, or seems excessively fizzy, just release the gas by opening the lid and make sure all the vegetables are submerged in liquid. Have a taste, and if it's ready to eat, put it in the refrigerator to slow the fermentation down.

TIP

When storing kimchi, it's a good idea to put the jar on a tray in case it overflows.

Chapter Three
Eating Kimchi
How to enjoy your kimchi

KIMCHI'S FLAVOUR PROFILE

Kimchi classically has a complex flavour profile that combines sourness, spiciness and umami.

SOUR

This makes it a great companion to rich foods that benefit from having something that cuts through, which is why it's great with fried food and rich meats like pork.

SPICY

The chilli heat is a great foil for avocado and melted cheese (hence the popularity of kimchi mac and cheese in the USA).

UMAMI

This deep savoury flavour comes from the seafood element, classically jeotgal, a paste made from fermented salted shrimps or other seafood. Fish sauce or miso can be good alternatives.

Umami is partly what makes kimchi addictive and enjoyable on its own.

Kimchi is great with (or on)...

Hot dogs

Egg-fried rice

Sausages and mashed potatoes

Scrambled eggs

Creamy pasta dishes

Cheeseburgers

Tacos

Quesadillas

Grilled cheese sandwiches

Noodle stir-fries

Roast sweet potatoes

Cheesy chips

Kimchijeon – Korean Kimchi Pancake

Kimchi pancakes (called *jeon* or *buchimgae*) are beloved by many Koreans, and are also a great way to introduce people to the delights of kimchi. They're usually made as one large pancake that is cut into wedges to serve, but you can make individual ones too.

INGREDIENTS

7 oz (200 g) baechu (cabbage) kimchi
2 spring onions (scallions), chopped
¼ tsp salt
¼ tsp sugar
1½ oz (45 g) plain flour
1½ oz (45 g) rice or corn flour (or double the plain flour)
½ tsp baking powder
1 tsp gochugaru (Korean chilli flakes) (optional)
1 tbsp vegetable oil

- Chop the kimchi, put it in a large bowl and stir in the spring onions (including the green parts), salt and sugar, both types of flour, baking powder and gochugaru (if using).
- Add enough cold water (or you could use kimchi brine) to make a fairly thick batter.
- Heat the vegetable oil in a heavy-based frying pan. Pour in enough batter to generously cover the base and cook for 2–3 minutes over medium heat, or until crispy and golden.
- Use a fish slice to turn the pancake over and cook the other side. Serve immediately.

Kimchi Jjigae – Winter Stew

This cold-weather warmer is a great way to use up kimchi that's turned a bit too sour or is past its best. Its sourness melds beautifully with the richness of pork belly, but you could use any cut of meat, or even replace the meat with sweet potatoes and hard-boiled eggs for a vegetarian version.

INGREDIENTS

Stew

4 lb (1.8 kg) pork belly joint, rolled and boneless
2 white onions, sliced
2¼ lb (1 kg) kimchi
1 pint (600 ml) chicken stock
4 tbsp mirin (rice wine)
10 oz (300 g) silken tofu, cubed
Spring onions, to serve

Paste

1½ tbsp light soy sauce
½ tbsp red or brown miso paste
½ tbsp gochujang (Korean chilli paste)
1½ tbsp honey
2 spring onions, finely chopped
2 garlic cloves, minced
¾ in (2 cm) fresh root ginger, finely chopped

- Mix together the paste ingredients and rub over the pork belly joint. Leave to marinate for a few hours (or overnight).
- Roast the pork, along with its marinade, in a medium-low oven (280°F/140°C/gas 1) for 2–3 hours, until tender.
- When the pork is ready, heat a little oil in a pan and gently cook the onions until they are soft, brown and caramelized (about 10–15 minutes).
- Add the kimchi and cook for a few minutes until sizzling.
- Pour in the chicken stock, mirin and any cooking juices from the pork and simmer.
- Cut the roasted pork into small chunks and add it to the kimchi pan.
- Simmer for 10 minutes, then add the tofu. Stir gently so as not to break up the tofu.
- Sprinkle with chopped spring onions and serve.

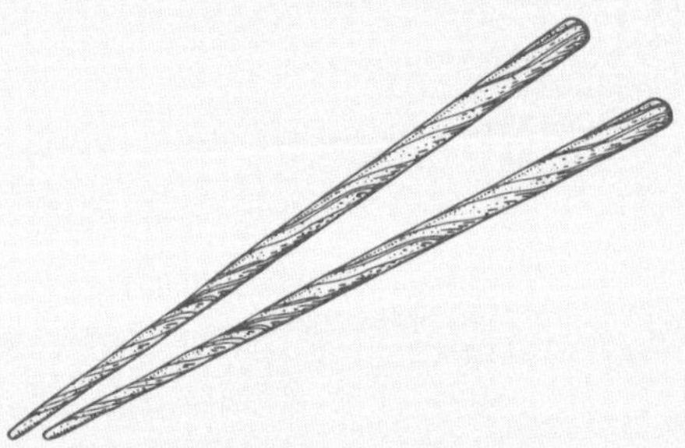

Kimchi Cream Cheese Dip

- Blend 2 tbsp kimchi with 5½ oz (150 g) cream cheese, 5½ oz (150 g) sour cream and 2 tsp soy sauce until smooth.
- Serve with your favourite crackers and crudités for an addictively moreish dip.

Kimchi Mac & Cheese

Next time you make mac and cheese, try adding a layer of chopped kimchi in the middle.

This works especially well alongside stronger cheeses like mature cheddar or gruyère.

Kimchi Heroes #3

The **Kimchi Warrior** is an animated character who gains supernatural strength from eating kimchi, and thus is able to save humanity from dire opponents like malaria, SARS and swine flu, all of which are summoned by the Evil Lord of Disease to wipe us out.

Having trained under the Kimchi Master, the Kimchi Warrior bravely uses special ingredient weapons to destroy her opponents.

She was developed by creator and director Young Man Kan in 2009 and released on YouTube. A second batch of episodes was ordered by the Korea Agro-Fisheries & Food Trade Corporation in 2011.

Kimchi Quesadillas

Kimchi is a great accompaniment to the rich, melty cheese of a quesadilla, especially alongside avocado and a squeeze of fresh lime juice. Add it to your next wrap!

KIMCHI BRINE

There are lots of good ways to use up any leftover kimchi brine (the liquid left in the jar once you've eaten the contents). Don't throw it down the sink!

- **Add it to a martini cocktail**
- **Use it to make a quick pickle with thinly sliced vegetables**
- **Use it as a dressing for a salad or coleslaw**
- **Toss it into noodles, especially alongside crispy pork belly**
- **Use it to lightly pickle eggs**
- **Toss it into rice for the base of an Asian-style salad**

Kimchi Tacos

Kimchi is great in soft flour tacos, alongside pulled pork shoulder, beef brisket, or cheese and avocado. Fresh coriander (cilantro) and sour cream are also great additions.

You could also try using Korean bulgogi (barbecued beef) as a delicious taco filling.

Kimchi Pizza

Kimchi can make an excellent pizza topping, especially alongside pepperoni or other rich, meaty toppings.

Finely chop it and mix with the cheese before cooking the pizza.

Alternatively, sprinkle over a pizza fresh out of the oven.

BUDAE JJIGAE – ARMY BASE STEW

This rich, savoury stew was created in the early 1950s when the American army was stationed in Uijeongbu, near Seoul, South Korea.

Army rations like spam, preserved Polish sausage, processed cheese and baked beans were combined with kimchi, gochujang and instant noodles (*ramyeon*) to create a nourishing stew beloved by Korean and US soldiers alike.

BANCHAN

Banchan are small dishes of vegetables, fish and meat that are served in the middle of the table for diners to share, along with the rice and soup or stew that make up most Korean meals.

They are traditionally served in groups of three, five, seven or nine dishes because odd numbers are considered good luck.

The term banchan is often translated as "side dishes", but they can be the main part of the meal.

Kimchi is generally not considered as banchan — it is an essential part of every meal.

Kimchi Ice Cream

Yes, people have made it!

- Simmer 2 tbsp kimchi to drive out the liquid, then puree with 1 tbsp honey and a large handful of fresh strawberries or raspberries.
- Strain this mixture through a sieve, then fold in 10 fl oz (300 ml) whipped cream and 14 fl oz (400 ml) condensed milk.
- Churn in an ice-cream machine and serve.

Say "kimchi"!

Did you know that, instead of saying "cheese" when having their photograph taken, Korean people usually say "kimchi"?

It stands to reason, considering the prevalence of kimchi over cheese in the local diet.

And the vocal muscles used to pronounce the word also coax the mouth into a camera-ready smile.

Kimchi Smoothie

Boost the gut-healthy properties of your favourite smoothie by adding a tablespoon of kimchi.

Try it with fresh spinach, strawberries, banana and pear for a taste sensation.

Kimchi & Spam Fried Rice

Kimchi and Spam are a legendary pairing. The crisp heat and sourness of the kimchi is perfect with salty, rich Spam. This recipe, inspired by US food writer J. Kenji Lopéz-Alt, is an absolute winner.

INGREDIENTS

3½ oz (100 g) kimchi
5½ oz (150 g) Spam
2 tsp vegetable oil
2 spring onions (scallions), chopped
1 garlic clove, finely chopped
1 red chilli, finely chopped (optional)
9 oz (250 g) cooked rice
Fried egg, hot sauce and chopped fresh coriander (cilantro), to serve

- Drain the kimchi, pressing to get rid of excess juice, and cut the Spam into cubes.
- Heat the oil in a frying pan, add the Spam and cook until starting to crisp.
- Add the spring onions, garlic and chilli (if using) and cook for 1 minute.
- Add the rice and cook, stirring, for 1 minute.
- Then add the kimchi and cook, stirring, for a further 2 minutes, or until everything is hot through, sizzling and crispy.
- Serve with a fried egg, hot sauce and some chopped coriander, if you like.

TIP

Use spicy sausage or bacon instead of Spam.

Kimchi Grilled Cheese Sandwich

Kimchi makes a fine combination with melted cheese.

- Take two slices of bread (preferably sourdough) and butter one side of each slice. Fill the non-buttered side with grated cheese (a mixture of mozzarella with cheddar or gruyère works well) and a layer of well-drained kimchi.
- Heat a heavy-based pan over low-medium heat and place the sandwich, buttered-side-down, in the pan.
- Allow to fry gently, pressing down occasionally with a spatula (or rest a weight on top). Flip it over after a minute or two to cook the other side. Both sides should be golden brown.
- Cut in half and serve immediately.

Kimchi Popcorn

Dehydrate some kimchi (using a dehydrator or bake in a very low oven for 12 hours).

Grind it to a powder and sprinkle over some freshly popped and buttered popcorn.

Next level!

"Kimchi is important like air is important."

Jung Eun Chae,
***Guardian*, 30 July 2024**